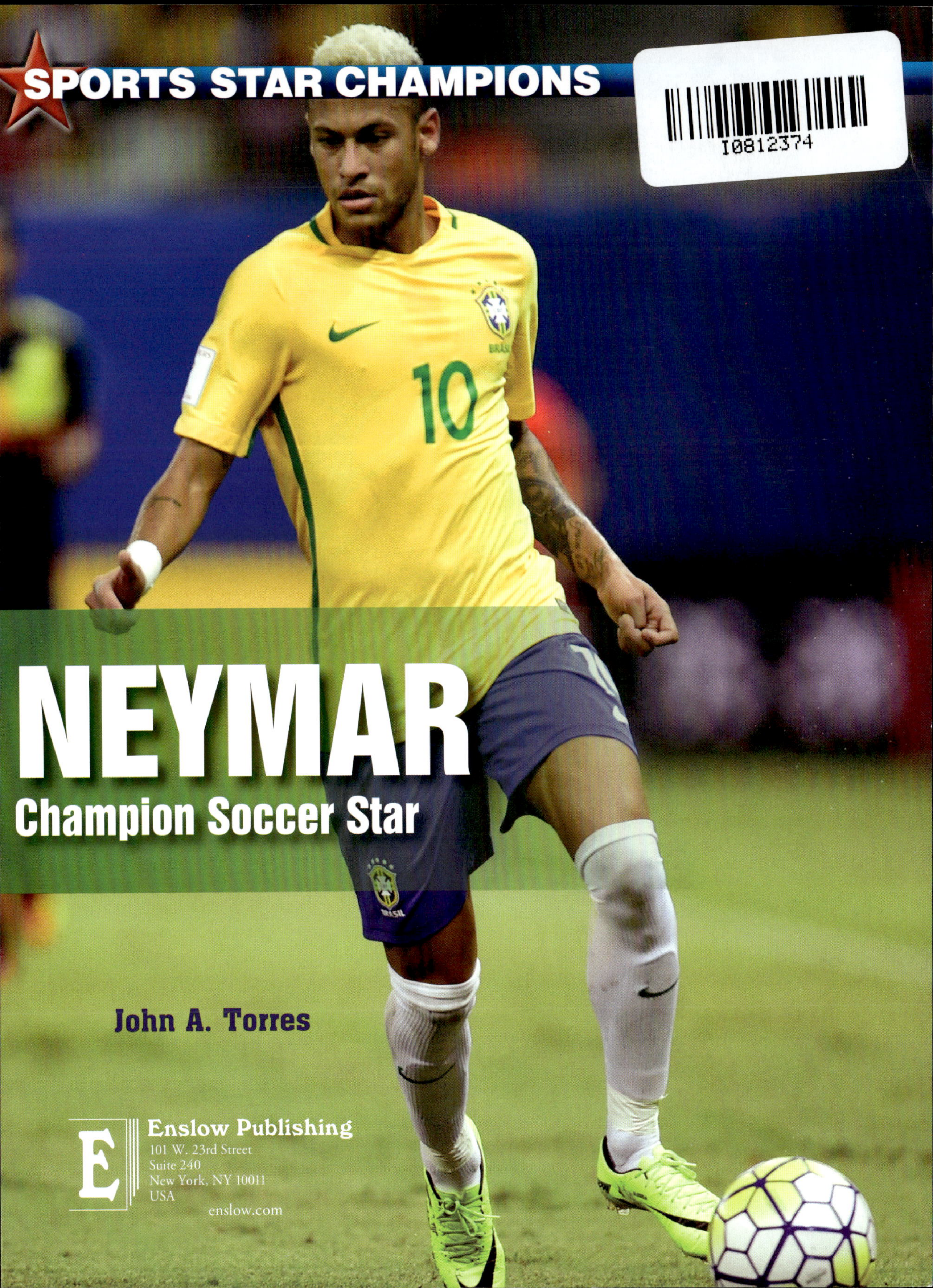

SPORTS STAR CHAMPIONS

NEYMAR

Champion Soccer Star

John A. Torres

Enslow Publishing
101 W. 23rd Street
Suite 240
New York, NY 10011
USA
enslow.com

Published in 2018 by Enslow Publishing, LLC.
101 W. 23rd Street, Suite 240, New York, NY 10011

Library of Congress Cataloging-in-Publication Data

Names: Torres, John Albert, author.
Title: Neymar : champion soccer star / John A. Torres.
Description: New York : Enslow Publishing, 2018. | Series: Sports Star Champions | Includes bibliographical references and index. | Audience: Grade 6-8.
Identifiers: LCCN 2017003411| ISBN 9780766086944 (library-bound) | ISBN 9780766087576 (pbk.) | ISBN 9780766087583 (6-pack)
Subjects: LCSH: Neymar, 1992---Juvenile literature. | Soccer players--Brazil--Biography--Juvenile literature.
Classification: LCC GV942.7.N455 T67 2018 | DDC 796.334092 [B] --dc23
LC record available at https://lccn.loc.gov/2017003411

Printed in the United States of America

To Our Readers: We have done our best to make sure all websites in this book were active and appropriate when we went to press. However, the author and the publisher have no control over and assume no liability for the material available on those websites or on any websites they may link to. Any comments or suggestions can be sent by email to customerservice@enslow.com.

Photo Credits: Cover, p. 1 Bruno Zanardo/Getty Images; pp. 4-5, 6 Simon Bruty /Sports Illustrated/ Getty Image; pp. 8, 12 Ricardo Nogueira/AFP/Getty Images; p. 10 NurPhoto Getty Images; p. 14 Tim Clayton/Corbis Sport/Getty Images; p. 17 Keiny Andrade/LatinContent WO/Getty Images; p. 18 Jamie McDonald/FIFA/Getty Images; pp. 21, 29, 39 David Ramos/Getty Images; p. 23 News Free/ Latin Content/Getty Images; p. 24 AFP/Getty Images; p. 27 Evaristo Sa/AFP/Getty Images; p. 30 Buda Mendes/Getty Images; p. 31 Jean Catuffe/Getty Images; p. 35 © AP Images; p. 37 Bob Thomas/ Popperfoto/Getty Images; pp. 40-41 Gonzalo Arroyo Moreno/Getty Images; p. 43 Manuel Blondeau/ Corbis Sport/Getty Images.

Contents

Introduction

They call soccer "the beautiful game" in Brazil. Sure, other sports like basketball and boxing are popular in the South American country, but soccer—or *futbol*—is king.

The country has produced legendary soccer players like Pelé, Didi, Ronaldinho, and countless others. The greats are usually known only by one name. And Neymar is no different. Even though he is still a very young player, only starting to hit his prime, he was able to accomplish something none of the greats before him ever did—lead Brazil to an Olympic gold medal.

Brazilian superstar Neymar takes the winning penalty kick against Germany during the gold medal game of the 2016 Olympics.

But what is it that makes a champion? Is it hard work? Natural talent? Dedication? Just luck? Well, it is likely a combination of all those things, but none is more important than hard work and dedication. Those are traits that all sports champions share.

Although Brazil has long been one of the world leaders of international soccer, the country had never won a gold medal. And things did not look promising in the summer of 2016 when the Brazilian Olympic team, led by Neymar, advanced to the gold medal game against Germany.

The Germans were the best international team in the world. Only two years earlier, during the 2014 World Cup in Brazil, the Germans destroyed the home team 7–1 during the World Cup semi-final match. It was a crushing defeat that left the team in disarray, and it seemed to scar, or at least shake, the nation's confidence.

But here were the two teams once again lined up against each other. This time the gold medal was at stake. The teams came out a bit tentatively, but it was Brazil—and Neymar—who struck first. It happened after a foul, a little more than thirty yards (twenty-seven meters) out and to the left of Germany's goalkeeper, Timo Horn.

It takes a great deal of skill to get the ball past a world-class keeper from thirty yards away. Most soccer players would opt instead to loft the ball into the box where one of his or her teammates could try to put the ball in with a header.

But Neymar is unlike most soccer players. He paused and then gave an exaggerated stutter step before swatting a dipping and curving line-drive shot just past Horn's outstretched hand. Brazil

Neymar and his teammates salute the fans with their newly won gold medals.

took a 1–0 lead. The stadium in Brazil went wild. People waved flags and chanted. Would this be the year that Brazil actually took home a gold medal?

But the Germans weren't ready to give up. They scored the equalizer, or tying goal, a short time after halftime, making it 1–1. That's when both teams decided to play very conservatively throughout the rest of the match and even throughout the overtime periods.

Still tied 1–1, the match went to penalty kicks. This is when teams line up to take five shots from close range against the keeper. Brazil saved Neymar for the last kick. It was 4–4 because one German player was unable to score. If Neymar could score, an entire nation would celebrate. He placed the ball down and took a few steps back. He paused, started running, stuttered, and almost stopped before burying the ball into the back of the net. Neymar had done it, and Brazil had finally won its gold medal.

1

Garbage Dump

Neymar da Silva Santos Jr. came into this world on February 5, 1992, in the very poor Mogi das Cruzes neighborhood of San Paolo—the capital of Brazil. His father, Neymar Santos Sr., had been a professional soccer player. His mother's name is Nadine da Silva.

The neighborhood was poor but not impoverished or violently unsafe, as some of the other more dangerous San Paolo neighborhoods are known to be. Many of the streets were not paved and the area did not have many buildings. The worst thing about the neighborhood was often the smell. Right behind the neighborhood was a garbage dump where many residents of the large, sprawling city would throw their trash. It was not very pleasant at times, but it was the only world the little boy knew. Neymar was lucky to be raised by loving parents.

Neymar grew up in this Brazilian neighborhood.

The young boy was also lucky that his father knew a thing or two about pursuing dreams and the kind of mentality needed to succeed. His father was a hard worker, too. In fact, despite having once been a professional soccer player, Neymar's father was very poor and had to work three jobs to be able to feed the family, which also included Neymar's younger sister, Rafaela. In fact, the family was so poor that they could not afford electricity. They lived by candlelight.

Luck was definitely with the family, and Neymar in particular one night when he was only four months old. His father was driving the family to visit relatives when it began pouring rain. His sister had not been born yet. The mountain roads can be dangerous, even during dry conditions, and this was a blinding rain. His father never saw the oncoming car until it was too late to maneuver. They collided, and Neymar's father's legs were mangled and twisted. Neymar's mother suffered some minor injuries but when they turned to check on Neymar, he was gone!

His parents panicked. Where was their little boy? Had he been thrown from the car?

"We couldn't find Neymar Jr. We thought the force of the impact had thrown him out of the car," his father would say years later during an interview. "I shudder every time I remember the moment. But who believes in God, has faith! The people who rescued us found our son under the seat of the car."

That's right. They looked for the baby everywhere but he was there the entire time, lying beneath the seat. He was covered in glass and was bleeding from numerous little cuts and one fairly deep gash on his forehead, but overall he was alright.

You can't say that Neymar was born with a soccer ball in his hands, but you wouldn't be too far off the mark. "My first ball was given to me by my mom when I was two years old," Neymar said, adding that eventually he had more than fifty soccer balls inside his house. "I used to drive my mom crazy."

The little boy didn't like anyone else to ever have his ball, so he started playing a version of "keep-away" from a very young age. By using his feet, he kept the ball away from anyone who was around. Neymar started to develop incredible ball dribbling and ball control skills, even as a toddler. It would serve him well in the years to come.

"The secret is to believe in your dreams."

—Neymar

"When I was small I didn't want anyone else to get the ball. I always wanted to score a goal," Neymar said. "At home, I would always be dribbling my ball around the chairs and the table." It certainly helped that his father had been a professional soccer player himself.

There weren't many soccer fields or youth leagues in the poor neighborhood where Neymar grew up. But that didn't keep the future champion soccer star from playing the game he loved so much. Instead, he and his friends played a game called *futsal*, which has become very popular in the streets of Latin America. It is very similar to soccer but features fewer players, and it is usually played indoors in a small area.

Neymar enjoys a close relationship with his father. Here, he shows off his soccer shin guards that are decorated with a photo of him and his father.

Futsal

The sport of futsal is a variation of soccer that is usually played indoors in gymnasiums or outdoors in schoolyards. The rules are similar to soccer except that there are only five players per team, including the goalkeeper. The ball is a little smaller and heavier than a standard soccer ball in order to keep it from bouncing too much. The game relies on players being creative and able to pass the ball in small spaces. The game was invented in 1930 by a teacher in Uruguay and became popular almost immediately. The game spread throughout all of South America and eventually the world.

In addition to futsal or indoor soccer, Neymar played street futbol, or soccer, whenever he could. Before he knew it, Neymar was better than just about everyone around and was often the first player chosen to a team during these pickup games. These games were also helping him develop the skills he would need.

"Indoor football was good at teaching me how to dribble with more speed. It also gave me a better, more concentrated view of the game," Neymar explained.

Putting soccer skills aside, the main thing that impressed Neymar's father was that his son was having fun. In fact, it looked as if he was the happiest boy out there playing soccer.

Neymar learned to dribble in tight places in part by playing *futsal*, or indoor soccer, like these young people are getting ready to play.

The stench from the nearby garbage dump didn't matter much when that smile was on Neymar's face! But Neymar Sr. also said it was very important not to push his child into becoming a soccer player. He wanted Neymar to be whatever he wanted to be.

"He was always a happy boy, like any other child. Innocent and always willing to have fun, to play too—mostly with a soccer ball though," his father recalled. "My wife and I always thought we had to let Neymar and his sister develop naturally, to truly have the choice to be happy. So as a child he wanted to be everything: Superman, Power Rangers. The kid was hyperactive—he still is today!"

Neymar's family provided him and his sister with a loving home, and they taught their children respect, humility, and faith. They are a very religious family. Those values have stuck with Neymar through the years.

"They are everything to me," Neymar said about his family. "They are my base; they help me in all that I need. I thank God for putting me in this family."

2

Family Move

When he was eleven years old, Neymar and his family moved to a new home away from the garbage dump. They moved to a wealthier area called Sao Vicente, which is closer to the coast. It was the first settlement the Portuguese made in the Americas. Nearby is a commercial port area known as Santos. Neymar started playing soccer on the sandy beaches, honing his skills and getting better every day.

It was there, in nearby Santos, that Neymar started playing organized soccer in a competitive youth league. Now, it's important to understand how things work in some countries. In Brazil, and many other soccer-crazed nations, many of the youth leagues are affiliated with or part of a larger professional team. Sometimes, the manager of the professional team will sign a youth player to a contract and he will continue training at the club with the goal of playing professionally for that team someday. Imagine playing Little League baseball and the New York Yankees signing you to a contract when you are still only a boy or girl. That's exactly what happened with Neymar.

Right from the start, it seemed that Neymar was destined for greatness. Here he is a young man playing for Santos FC in 2010.

The coaches at Santos Futbol Club liked Neymar so much that they signed him to a contract. They also took Neymar and his younger sister out of a very bad public school and paid for them to go to private school, where they flourished.

Neymar was known as a great student with a lot of energy and respect for his teachers. But there was one class he was having trouble with—physical education! That was because it took place at the same time that Neymar had practice with his team from Santos. The other kids at the school who played for the school's soccer team complained to their teacher.

So, one day Neymar had permission to skip practice with Santos and instead showed up to soccer practice at the school. He was so far advanced and ahead of every other student that he put on a soccer clinic. He dribbled the ball through their legs, around them, and even flicked the ball up and over their heads and scored one goal after another. He was able to score at will. Needless to say that neither his teacher nor his classmates ever complained again about him missing physical education class at school.

Even though he was barely thirteen years old, Neymar had signed a contract and was making money for his family. Combined with the money that his father was earning at his jobs, the family was now earning enough to buy their first house in a very nice neighborhood. The family's quality of life improved drastically. It made Neymar proud to be able to help his family.

"I was able to give back to them what they did for me," he would later say.

He advanced quickly through the ranks for Santos and when he was only fifteen years old, Neymar played in the 2008 Copa Sao Paulo—a prestigious youth soccer tournament for those under the age of eighteen. He was one of the youngest players to participate and was regarded as an up-and-coming player.

"I have to enjoy every moment."
—Neymar

He impressed coaches from all over who had come to see him play, and he was even being compared to some of the all-time greats. One of his first coaches described Neymar's style of play as having an almost musical quality to it, with an element that is not only rare but hard to describe.

"Of all the boys I dealt with, none of them had what Neymar has," his coach said. "He moves fast. He has the facility to trick the opponent, to dribble, moving your own body. He has this 'thing' that's something Brazilians are born with."

But there was still just a little something missing. Neymar, who was tall and spindly, seemed to lack the strength that

Neymar celebrates a goal for Santos. He is known as an emotional player who loves to celebrate his goals.

some of the other boys had. He was too skinny. So the trainers at Santos FC put him on a special diet to help him gain some weight and bulk up a little.

Whatever they did worked. Because the following year, as a sixteen-year-old playing in the Copa Sao Paulo, Neymar scored three goals and was clearly the best player around. His performance was so terrific that Brazil's under-seventeen national team wanted him to play and represent the country in an international competition. But his team wanted him to have more club experience first. The hype around Neymar was starting to build.

Neymar fights for the ball during a FIFA U-17 World Cup match between Brazil and Japan in 2009.

And Pelé, possibly the best soccer player who ever lived, exclaimed to a magazine at the time that Neymar "could be better than me."

The next year was Neymar's first as a true professional soccer player. He scored more than ten goals and was earning a reputation as a crafty and imaginative playmaker who had the ability to make everyone on the field better. This time when the national team came calling, his managers had to say yes. The teenager would be representing Brazil in the U-17 World Cup!

There was talk that perhaps the national team would ask Neymar to join the men's team and play in the 2010 FIFA World Cup. But that call never came. And if being left off the team bothered the youngster, he never let it show.

World Cup

Started in 1930, the World Cup is held every four years. It is the most prestigious soccer tournament in the world and consists of senior men's national teams from countries all over the world. During the four years between World Cups, national teams play in various tournaments and qualifying matches to earn enough points to qualify for the World Cup.

There have been twenty World Cup tournaments. It was cancelled twice during World War II. Brazil has won it five times. Germany and Italy have each won it four times. It is the most watched sporting event in the world.

Neymar especially never let it show on the field of play. He was named best player in the state championship that season and finished as top scorer of the Copa do Brasil. Then in December 2011, he was named to the Brazilian championship team of the year, a type of all-star honor.

Even though he wouldn't be playing in the World Cup, the national team did reward him by asking him to play in an international match against the United States in August 2010. How did he respond? Neymar scored his first international goal and led Brazil to a 2–0 victory. As a teenager, his dreams were already coming true.

3

Superstar

Though he wasn't really an overnight sensation, to soccer fans around the world who don't particularly follow Brazilian soccer, Neymar seemed to rise to stardom overnight. Suddenly his name was on the lips of coaches and fans of the English Premier League, Spain's La Liga, Italy's Serie A, and Germany's Bundesliga. Those are regarded by soccer experts as the four best leagues in the world. The most talented players normally wind up playing for one of the top four European leagues.

And Neymar nearly wound up there as a young man. When he was only fourteen years old he was already being scouted by some of the best teams in the world. One of those teams, Real Madrid of Spain, actually flew Neymar and his father to Spain for a tryout.

Real Madrid is one of the best teams in the world and it is where Portuguese legend Cristiano Ronaldo has played for many years. After watching the teenager train for just three days, the owners of Real Madrid offered Neymar a contract. It was a deal similar to the one that Barcelona gave Leo Messi as a teen as well.

It would make Neymar and his family rich and ensure that his career would follow a path set forth by one of the best teams in the world. Neymar would, of course, have to move to Spain and continue his training and his education there. But there were some things to consider. The culture in Spain is very different from that of Brazil, and Neymar would also have to learn to speak a new language. Although Portuguese, spoken in Brazil, and Spanish, spoken in Spain, are very similar, there would still be a steep learning curve. He would also miss his family, with whom he is very close.

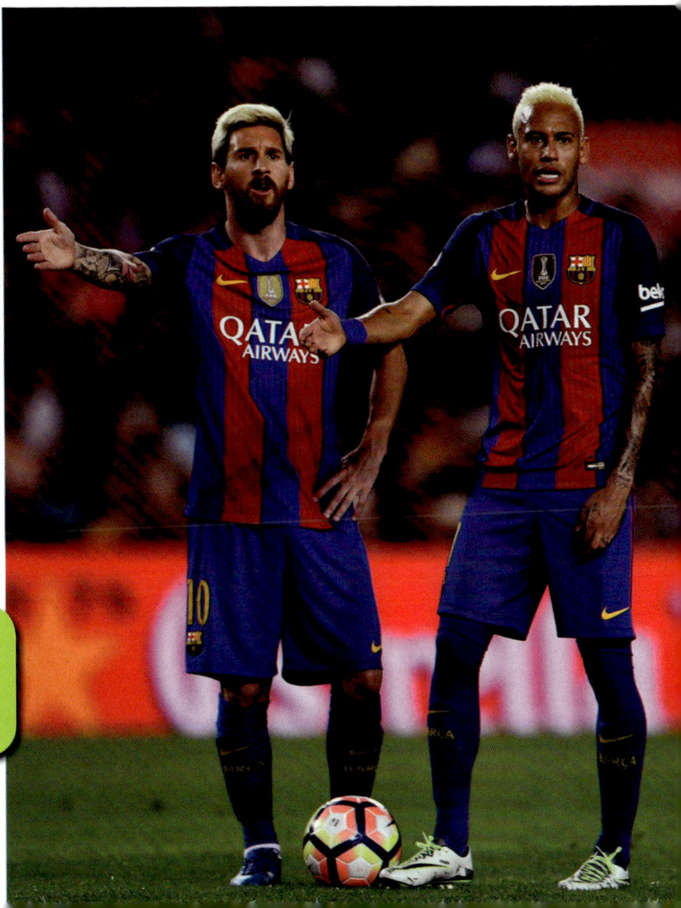

Barcelona FC boasts two of the best players in the world—Leo Messi (*left*) and Neymar (*right*).

Neymar stayed for only ten days before announcing he wanted to go home because he was too homesick. For now, Neymar, the teenager, was content playing on his home turf. He did not know it at the time but Neymar would become even more popular in Brazil as news that he rejected Real Madrid traveled around the country.

"After I turned down the offer from Real Madrid in 2006, everyone knew who I was," Neymar said. "And after that, even when playing for the youth team, I had at least one request per game for photographs from the fans. That was not normal for someone my age. But I had to get used to it."

His father, always there to guide and help him, reminded his son that not even the great Pelé had so much attention on him as a youth player.

The move to turn down Real Madrid worked out just fine for the young man. He continued working hard, training, and advancing through the ranks of Santos. Just a few years later he helped his club win two consecutive championships—the Copa do Brasil and the 2011 Copa Liberatadores—which marked the first time Santos FC had won a continental title since 1963.

By 2010, the eighteen-year-old was winning just about every honor offered in Brazilian soccer. On April 15 of that year, he scored an amazing five goals in one match to lead Santos to the qualifying stages of the Brazilian Cup. In another tournament that season, Neymar scored fourteen goals in nineteen matches, and he was given an award for being the best player in the competition. The offers from top clubs in Europe continued pouring in. It wouldn't be long before the youngster took his game one step higher to the highest levels of competition.

Neymar holds the trophy for best player of the Copa Santander Libertadores in 2011 in Brazil.

In 2011 and 2012, Neymar continued making his mark on professional and international soccer. His club, Santos, renegotiated his contract and made him the highest-paid player in South America. Most of the South American teams cannot afford to hold onto their superstars because the European clubs can pay them so much more.

In 2011, Neymar was awarded the best footballer in South America award as a teenager. And things would only get better. In 2012, on his twentieth birthday, Neymar scored his one hundredth goal as a professional! Most players do not

Neymar (*far left*) dances with teammates after scoring a goal in 2012 for Santos FC.

score one hundred goals in their entire careers. During this time, Neymar had to continuously deny rumors that he was leaving Brazil to play in Europe.

That March and April, Neymar went on a spectacular scoring spree. He scored three goals—or a hat trick—to help Santos beat Internacional 3–1. He scored two goals apiece in victories against Guarani and another brace—two goals—in a victory against Guaratingueta. He was once again voted the best player in South America, and this forced him to make a decision.

Hat Trick

The sports world is filled with many colorful terms. One of those is "hat trick." This refers primarily to soccer or ice hockey when a player scores three goals in a single game.

There are many different legends about how the term got started. Some believe hockey teams would offer fans free hats if a player scored three goals. Others believe it was a collection taken up in a hat for a cricket player who scored three times. But these days it is not unusual to see hats come flying down from the stands onto the ice during a hockey match or the pitch during a soccer game to celebrate the accomplishment.

He had already won just about every award he could in South America. He also led his club, Santos, to several titles and tournament victories. There was very little else for him to accomplish. So, with an excited but heavy heart, Neymar decided to leave Brazil and pursue his career in Spain with Barcelona FC, one of the most talented teams in the world, which already boasted arguably the best player in the world, Leo Messi. They would go on to later add superstar Luis Suarez to their roster.

> **"Sorry, I can't stop scoring."**
> —*Neymar*

It was revealed later that the offer Barcelona made to both Neymar and Santos was one of the highest ever in the sport. It was the culmination of a fierce two-year bidding war with Barcelona's rival Real Madrid. It would also be an opportunity to make more money than he had ever imagined.

On May 26, 2013, just before his final match as a member of Santos, Neymar stood on the sidelines, listened to the national anthem, and cried. Later on, he told reporters that he was very happy that Barcelona had made his dream come true.

Neymar gets emotional before the start of his final game for Santos. His next game would be for soccer powerhouse Barcelona.

"I am very grateful that Barcelona did what it had to do to complete my childhood, to be with my idols," he said, mentioning Messi in particular. "I am very happy, very moved to be a Barcelona player and fulfill my dream. I want to help the team. I have come to add my part so that Lionel Messi continues to be the best player in the world."

4

Comparisons

There would be no homesickness this time around. Neymar left his homeland for the chance to play for one of the best and most respected teams in the world.

Certainly the competition in Europe would be fiercer than what Neymar faced in Brazil. The only question was whether he was up to the challenge. He certainly couldn't get more famous or more well-known, could he?

Even before signing the massive contract with Barcelona, Neymar was one of the most recognizable athletes in the world. He was featured on the covers of video games, such as Pro Evolution Soccer 2012 and Pro Evolution Soccer 2013. He also became the first athlete ever to be featured on the cover of *Time* magazine, where he was again compared to Pelé. He even became a featured character in a Brazilian comic book for kids.

His soccer skills, boyish charm, and good looks broadened his appeal to go way beyond the soccer world. In 2013, *Sportspro* magazine called Neymar the most marketable athlete on the planet, something it did in 2012 as well. That meant he topped athletes like golfer Rory McIlroy, American football star Tom Brady, and even Jamaican track sensation Usain Bolt.

Neymar gets airborne to head a ball into the net during the Copa del Rey in 2013.

Neymar shows off his new Nike cleats in 2013 in Brazil. Neymar is a spokesman for many products.

Neymar has interests outside of soccer, too. He remains a huge fan of Brazilian music and sometimes coordinates his celebratory dances to help promote a friend's new music recording. He once did a music video in the locker room of his Santos club after a match. He danced and held a radio to his ear while trying to get teammates to dance. Neymar has also become a spokesman for Nike and Panasonic. He is active on social media and boasts more than fifty million Facebook fans.

On a personal note, Neymar is very religious. He is a Christian who reportedly donates 10 percent of everything he makes to the church. He is also very involved in charitable work to help the poor. Every year without fail, he teams up with fellow Brazilian soccer star Nene to organize a charity soccer match to raise money for food to help poor families in Brazil.

His family remains important to him. Neymar is still very close to his parents and has a strong bond with his sister Rafaella. He even has her image tattooed on his arm. Before signing with Barcelona, Neymar experienced the joy of fatherhood when his child, Davi Lucca, was born. He is widely quoted as saying he was initially terrified at the thought of being a father.

"I cried when I learned that I would be his father," he said. "At first, I felt fear. Then joy. It is a new responsibility and I am now enjoying it."

Neymar enjoys a moment with his son after helping Brazil win the gold medal against Germany during the 2016 Olympics.

For the 2013–14 soccer season, Barcelona wanted to ease Neymar into the competition and the flow of the games without overwhelming him. He was brought along slowly, even as a substitute late in matches just to help him get used to his new team. They also wanted him to gain some weight and bulk up just a bit. The rigors of European soccer can certainly take their toll, and Neymar has always had a very slender frame. They wanted to make sure he would not suffer injuries or get too burned out during his first season. But even though the time spent on the pitch during that first season at Barcelona was minimal, Neymar made the most of it.

What really helps to set Neymar apart from other great soccer players is his true versatility. He excels at virtually every single position that his coaches ask him to play. So, exactly what is his position? Well, that can be hard to pin down. Sometimes Neymar is lined up as the central striker and sometimes he is lined up as a second striker. He also lines up as an attacking midfielder, which allows him all the freedom he needs to help create his amazing goals and assists. He has even lined up as a winger, typically a player who plays both offense and then runs all the way back downfield to play defense in front of his own net.

He shoots mainly with his right foot but has become adept at shooting with his left foot as well. For all his natural talents and accolades, like "explosive" and "electric," Neymar is also known as one of the hardest-working players in his sport. He knows that natural talent can only get him so far without the sweat and determination it takes to become a legend.

Leo Messi

Leo, or Lionel, Messi is Neymar's teammate at Barcelona and a fellow South American. Messi was born in Argentina and is regarded by many as the best player in the world.

Nicknamed "the Flea" because of his small size, Messi was born with a genetic deficiency that causes dwarfism. When he was only twelve years old, Barcelona signed him to a contract and said they would pay for the treatments he would need to be able to grow to average height.

Other teams have tried to lure Messi away from Barcelona, but he has said that he would like to play his entire career with just one team.

"I'm always trying to perfect everything—dribbling, shooting, headers, and control. You can always improve."

—Neymar

He often scored goals or assisted on others to help Barcelona stay atop the standings. It wouldn't be long before the club would remove the "training wheels" and let him do his thing. He scored nine goals in twenty-six appearances during the 2013–2014 season but increased the number to twenty-two goals in thirty-three appearances the following year. That's when the comparisons really started.

The better Neymar performs on the soccer field, the more people continue to compare him to Pelé and even teammate Leo Messi. Though he is flattered by the comparisons, they can also make him uncomfortable. But even Pelé was quoted once as saying he felt Neymar was better than Messi.

"Now everyone is talking about Messi; he is a star. But he must first become better than Neymar," Pelé said. "At the moment Messi is just more experienced."

But Neymar responded by being humble and only praising Messi, his teammate.

Neymar shares a laugh with retired soccer legend Pelé, who is regarded by many as the best soccer player in history.

"Messi is above everyone, there is no use comparing me with him," he said. "He is the best player in the world and I always get inspired when I watch good football."

In fact, Neymar said that his goal was to be more like Messi.

"I am a Messi fan. I support him to score a lot of nice goals so I can keep copying and imitating him," he said.

It won't be long before fellow superstars are saying the same thing about Neymar.

5

Champion

"To win the Ballon d'Or is a consequence of your work."

—Neymar

To call Neymar a champion would be an understatement. He has won titles and been parts of championship clubs much of his playing career. But the 2015–16 season was really one for the record books. A year before leading his country to the gold medal in the 2016 Olympics, the ultimate mark of a champion, Brazilian superstar Neymar led his club team—Barcelona—to historic new heights. For that season at least, the combination of Neymar, Leo Messi, and Luis Suarez would prove to be too much for any team in the world to handle.

Luis Suares (*left*), Leo Messi (*center*) and Neymar (*right*) form the most dangerous scoring trio in professional soccer today. The three players have led Barcelona FC to numerous championships.

The three magnificent scorers checked off the first hurdle of the team's historic year on May 17 when a 1–0 victory against Atletico Madrid clinched the La Liga championship title. This is not easy to do, especially for a club like Barcelona, which is so good that it qualified for other major tournaments at the same time. This means the team often plays multiple games a week, unlike the normal once-a-week schedule.

So, while the team was securing enough points to win the La Liga championship, Neymar and his teammates were also playing against the best teams in Europe in the hotly contested and very prestigious Champions League.

Neymar scored a spectacular second-half goal in early May to seal a hard-fought victory against Bayern Munich, often regarded as Germany's best team and one of the best in the world. A week later Neymar scored twice in a Champions League match against Allianz Arena that clinched a spot in the Champions League final.

But that wasn't all that was going on. The club was also participating in and advancing through the Copa del Rey—an annual soccer tournament consisting of all the teams in Spain, a country that has several professional soccer leagues. The tournament is long and grueling, especially for a team like Barcelona, which was struggling to win the La Liga title as well as the Champions League.

So, only one week after clinching the La Liga championship, Neymar scored the second goal of a 3–1 victory against Athletic Bilbao in the 2015 Copa del Rey final. During the closing moments of the match, Neymar was so happy that he started performing tricks with the ball and was accused by some members of the opposing

Neymar jumps for joy as he celebrates after scoring a goal during a Copa del Rey final match for Barcelona against Athletic Bilbao.

team of not showing good sportsmanship. Barcelona's manager, Luis Enrique, defended his star player by saying that Neymar's behavior at the end of the match is accepted in Brazil and that he was merely expressing his joy.

The criticism didn't bother Neymar one bit.

A little more than one week later Neymar and his teammates took the pitch in the Champions League final against the best team in Italy—Juventus. With the score 2–1 in favor of Barcelona in the second half, Neymar put the match out of reach by scoring a third goal and clinching the victory. This meant that Barcelona was now the only club in the history of professional soccer to win a "treble" twice. A treble is when a team wins its league championship, a domestic cup, and an international cup all in the same season.

Having previously won the Copa Libertadores, Neymar became only the eighth player in history to win the Copa Libertadores and the Champions League. He is also the only player in history to score goals during the final championship matches of both tournaments.

Neymar tallied thirty-nine goals that season. His teammates Messi and Suarez would account for an additional eighty-three goals. This meant the 122 goals the trio scored made them the most prolific front line in Spanish soccer history.

Remember, one year later he also brought the Olympic gold medal to Brazil after a hard-fought victory against Germany. There are no statistics to verify it, but Neymar is likely the only player in the world to have ever won a treble and a gold medal within twelve months.

Neymar was initially slowed by the mumps during the following season in Barcelona, but he rebounded from the illness in time to help his team win a second consecutive La Liga title and Copa Del Rey. Barcelona came up short in its defense of the Champions League title.

Score! Neymar puts in a goal for Barcelona during a 2015 match.

Perhaps the only accolade that has so far eluded the young Brazilian superstar is winning the Ballon d'Or, French for the Golden Ball. This award is given annually to the player regarded as the best soccer player from one of the European leagues, known as the best in the world. It is vey prestigious and extremely hard to win. In 2015, Neymar was listed as a finalist for the award. During the last several seasons the winners have been Messi and Real Madrid's Cristiano Ronaldo.

Ballon d'Or

The Ballon d'Or, or Golden Ball, is the highest individual honor awarded to professional soccer players participating in European soccer leagues. It is given to only one player every season. This means that the best players in the top leagues, such as Spain's La Liga, compete for the award with players from the English Premier League, Italy's Serie A, and Germany's Bundesliga.

In what is perhaps the ultimate testament to how great and competitive Spain's soccer league is, all the players to win the award since 2009 play in Spain.

While Neymar's goal in soccer has always been to try to win championships for his club and teammates, he does admit that winning the Ballon d'Or would be nice one day.

"I am very happy at Barcelona, in the team, with the life that I have," Neymar told a reporter in 2016. "Sure, I have the objective of winning the Ballon d'Or, but I will not die for it."

He went on to say that soccer—or football as it is referred to in Europe—brings him a lot of joy. He feels that joy translates into great play on the field. And he never thinks of personal awards when he is feeling that joy.

Neymar shares his joy for his sport with teammate and friend Leo Messi.

"I want to be happy and here I am happy. If I don't win the Ballon d'Or; no worries," he said. "I don't play football to win the Ballon d'Or, I play football to be happy. Because I enjoy it, and I want to play football."

Stats, Honors, and Records

STATS AND RECORDS

Club	Season	League		Cup		Continental		Intercontinental		Other		Total	
		Apps	Goals	Apps	Goals	Apps	Goals	Apps	Goals	Apps	Goals	Apps	Goals
Brazil		Brasileirão		Copa do Brasil		Continental		Club World Cup		Paulista		Total	
Santos	2009	33	10	3	1	–		–		12	3	48	14
	2010	31	17	8	11	2	0	–		19	14	60	42
	2011	21	13	–		13	6	2	1	11	4	**47**	**24**
	2012	17	14	–		14	9	–		16	20	**47**	**43**
	2013	1	0	4	1	–		–		18	12	**23**	**13**
	Total	**103**	**54**	**15**	**13**	**29**	**15**	**2**	**1**	**76**	**53**	**225**	**136**
Spain		La Liga		Copa del Rey		Europe		Club World Cup		Supercopa de España		Total	
Barcelona	2013–14	26	9	3	1	10	4	–		2	1	41	15
	2014–15	33	22	6	7	12	10	–		–		51	39
	2015–16	34	24	5	4	9	3	1	0	0	0	49	31
	Total	**93**	**55**	**14**	**12**	**31**	**17**	**1**	**0**	**2**	**1**	**141**	**85**
Career total		**208**	**113**	**29**	**25**	**65**	**34**	**3**	**1**	**78**	**54**	**383**	**227**

Individual Honors

World Soccer Young Player of the Year, 2011
Brazilian Silver Ball, 2010, 2011
Brazilian Golden Ball, 2011
FIFA Club World Cup Bronze Ball, 2011
South American Footballer of the Year, 2011, 2012
Copa Libertadores MVP, 2011
FIFA Confederations Cup Golden Ball, 2013
FIFA Confederations Cup Bronze Shoe, 2013
FIFA Confederations Cup Dream Team, 2013
FIFA World Cup Bronze Boot, 2014
FIFA World Cup Dream Team, 2014
Samba Gold, 2014, 2015,
FIFA FIFPro World XI 2015

Individual Records

Copa do Brasil Top scorer, 2010
South American Youth Championship Top scorer, 2011
Campeonato Paulista Top scorer, 2012
Copa Libertadores, tied for top scorer, 2012
UEFA Champions League, tied for top scorer, 2014–15

Chronology

1992 Neymar is born in San Paolo, Brazil.

1997 Starts playing for Santos FC youth team.

2006 Signs professional contract with Santos.

2007 Scores his first hat trick.

2011 Produces the FIFA Goal of the Year.

2012 Scores his one hundredth career goal on his twentieth birthday.

2012 Leads Brazil to silver medal in the Olympics.

2013 Signs lucrative deal with Barcelona.

2013 Leads Brazil to Confederations Cup Championship.

2014 Gets injured during World Cup.

2014–15 Leads Barcelona to numerous championships.

2016 Sits out the Copa America at the request of his Barcelona club, and Brazil flounders without him. Barcelona did not want him to get burned out by playing in too many tournaments.

2016 Wins elusive gold medal as he leads Brazil to Olympic championship.

Glossary

adept To be very good at something.

commercial Something used for business purposes.

consecutive One after another; back-to-back.

consequence The result of an action.

dedication An unveiling of something meant to honor a person or a thing.

flattered Feeling honored or pleased by someone's words.

flourished To prosper, thrive, and improve.

futsal An indoor version of soccer played in South America.

gash A deep cut.

grueling Something very difficult to finish.

impoverished Very poor.

massive Something very huge.

renegotiated To redo a previous agreement.

spindly Tall and very thin.

Further Reading

Books

Caioli, Lucia. *Neymar: The Unstoppable Rise of Barcelona's Brazilian Superstar.* London, UK: Icon Books, 2016.

Jokulsson, Illugi. *Neymar: The New Pelé.* New York, NY: Abbeville Press, 2015.

Logothetis, Paul. *Cristiano Ronaldo: International Soccer Star.* Edina, MN: ABDO Publishing, 2015.

Part, Michael. *Neymar: The Wizard.* Beverly Hills, CA: Sole Books, 2014.

WEBSITES

ESPN FC

espnfc.us/player/132948/neymar

This ESPN site features statistics, news, and information about Neymar.

Neymar Official Fan Site

neymaroficial.com/en

This is Neymar's official website, featuring profiles, news, stats, and features about him.

Index